Buenos Dias!
A Kid's Guide To Puerto Vallarta

Photography by John D. Weigand
Poetry by Penelope Dyan

Bellissima Publishing, LLC
Jamul, California
www.bellissimapublishing.com

Copyright © 2017 by Penny D. Weigand and John D. Weigand

All rights reserved. No part of this book may be reproduced or transmitted in any form or by any means, electronic or mechanical, including photocopying, recording, or by any other means, or by any information or storage retrieval system, without permission from the publisher.

ISBN 978-1-61477-270-5
First Edition

"My soul is full of longing
for the secret of the sea,
and the heart of the great ocean
sends a thrilling pulse through me."

Henry Wadsworth Longfellow

Buenos Días!
Bellissima Publishing, LLC

Introduction

Puerto Vallarta is a beautiful, tropical beach resort on the Pacific Ocean's Bahía de Banderas where you can see palm trees, shop, and swim in the beautiful blue waters and eat fish tacos to your content, even if it doesn't happen to be taco Tuesday! Puerto Vallarta was a thriving Mexican village long before it was a prime tourist destination. Tourism has been a success here, because of Puerto Vallarta's climate, scenery, tropical beaches, and rich cultural history, full of displays of art and culture you can see displayed right on its streets! There is also archaeological evidence suggesting continuous human habitation from 580 BC!

Written by award winning author, attorney, and former teacher, Penelope Dyan, this book is meant to entertain and teach, as children practice their reading skills. And the beautiful photographs taken by John D. Weigand perfectly compliment this fun book, giving kids a glimpse of what they might see and do on a visit to this beautiful place!

To see more of Puerto Vallarta, watch the fun, free music video that goes with this book on the Bellissimavideo YouTube channel.

Buenos Días!
Bellissima Publishing, LLC

Buenos Dias!
A Kid's Guide To Puerto Vallarta

Photography by John D. Weigand
Poetry by Penelope Dyan

You think, "Puerto Vallarta,
is the place to be!"
as you look down
upon its white sandy beaches,
and the blue of its sea!

Along the water's path you can walk.
And you can take a pause
to sit and to talk!

It's a very tropical place
that from San Diego, California
isn't very far.
And you can get there quite easily
by airplane, boat or car!

There are four grand stone arches
outlining the blue of the sky,
a symbol for ALL to see!
They mark the way
to the Los Arcos Amphitheater
where concerts,
cultural performances,
and other impromptu activities,
(throughout the year)
are free!

The famous three dolphin sculpture
marks the way
to the Pacific Ocean below,
where you can swim and play.
And if YOU are lucky
it might come true,
that you could be joined in YOUR swim
by a dolphin or two!

There are street vendors,
and music and entertainment
and shop after shop!
But when YOU see
THESE colorful
and costumed entertainers,
YOU just HAVE to stop!

And then, of course,
you MUST stop and stare,
and perhaps even buy
some of THIS artist's ware!

You find a shop
where you can buy lots of things!
You and Dad each get ONE T-shirt.
Your mom buys TWO necklaces,
with matching bracelets!
And THEN she buys THREE rings!

And then. . . after ALL of that,
(at an outdoor stand)
you and your father
EACH buy a hat!

The Church of Our Lady of Guadalupe
is beautiful inside!
And from its colorful beauty
you cannot hide.
Mom reminds you,
"There is more than beauty
to this place;
because it is filled with love,
and with God's grace!"

You see the
"Boy on the Seahorse" statue!
And to YOU it is like a dream,
of a magical place in the sea
that has NEVER been seen.
It is a place where boys and girls
swim with the fishes,
where hopes come true
along WITH wishes. . .
a place of love, peace and harmony,
that lives in dreams beneath the sea.
And YOU decide, if it is up to YOU,
that YOU will make
those dreams come true!

Weary and tired,
after a day of what seems like
a long fiesta,
you decide, like this street vendor,
it is TIME for a siesta!
And Dad also decides that it is best,
to give Mom a break
from her shopping,
and to give his wallet a rest!

Life is really simple,
but we insist
on making it complicated.

Confucius

www.ingramcontent.com/pod-product-compliance
Ingram Content Group UK Ltd.
Pitfield, Milton Keynes, MK11 3LW, UK
UKHW060132240426

12048UKWH00002B/10